Money & Marketing:
Social Profit Biz Basics

*Everything I Needed In Business I
Learned in the Bathroom*

Money & Marketing: Social Profit Biz Basics

Everything I Needed In Business I Learned in the Bathroom

Thyonne Gordon, Ph.D

First Printing: 2014

ISBN 978-1-889210-08-7 PAPERBACK
ISBN 978-1-889210-09-4 ELECTRONIC

A Writer Space dba
Beyond Story
4859 W. Slauson Ave. #299
Los Angeles, CA 90056

www.awriterspace.com
www.beyondstory.com

This book is dedicated to networkers and marketers who
market & fundraise with
FORTITUDE
Sustaining causes that matter

Molly Ann Mroczynski, M&M Philanthropy Consulting
Lee Rosenblum, Fundraising Professional
Cherie Carter, Development Director
Adam Pilder, Fundraising Professional – Major Gifts
Cynthia Heard, VP Communications & Advocacy YWCA GLA
Beverly Jackson, Social Marketing Professional

Contents

Introduction

Social Profit Biz Basics make it easy to recognize key elements that are necessary for any organization to survive – and in this series we learn it all from bathroom basics. Book one taught the basics of Infrastructure and led the reader on a course to have a solid foundation. Bare bones are important in business just like the bare bone essentials are important in a bathroom – a toilet and a sink will get you started just as quickly as a mission and a vision in an organization.

In book two we covered *People and Programs* and the lessons we found correlating to bathroom metaphors. One of the biggest lessons was on keeping the organization in flow – just like the flow of water we find in the bathroom.

Now, book three takes us on a journey to understand how bathrooms are built and maintained. We ask questions like what keeps the water flowing, the sinks clean and the shower with a constant and powerful stream?

Money & Marketing: Social Profit Biz Basics

The answer is in Money and Marketing. This book will guide you through learning tools that Social Profits use to market and bring money into organizations for sustainable growth.

As I began my career in the business world, I found many of my lessons came straight from the bathroom. Partly because it's a good place to reflect quietly and also because, there is so much to learn from its' inner workings.

These lessons would come as small metaphors yielding giant principles. The principles would guide me in reaching and teaching people as well as managing and maintaining processes. Eventually they would become a constant "go to" management tool.

Using the simple lessons in *Social Profit Biz Basics Money & Marketing: Everything I Needed To Know In Business, I Learned In the Bathroom,* will guide you into effective ways to market your service organization into the prosperous space you desire.

The book is divided into 3 parts using concepts and ideas straight from the bowels of the bathroom. You will learn key principles about Money and Marketing for your social profit including building a Case for Support, Sharing the Message and Securing Your Donors. It's an easy read and quite frankly, you can finish it behind a closed door, on a familiar seat. Yes! This is great bathroom reading material. Enjoy!

Author's Position

In this world where business is measured by the Dow and Wall Street status or how much companies make and take, I believe a shift must occur. This shift is based on the heart of a business. I know, many might note "business" as an entity does not have a heart. I say that every business is a creative energy of people and does have a heart.

With every client that's served, dollar that's earned and vendor that's affiliated, a steady beat occurs that gives the business a conscious how and why existence. And the beats are measured such that when there is a misstep, it causes a skip in that beat – and accordingly damage to that heart and ultimately to the business overall.

When we begin to focus on what value there is in giving goods and services as well as what we receive in return, we can grasp what a company's heart beat feels like. The idea is not so far-fetched. The giving begins with offering quality products and services for reasonable and fair pricing. However, it extends to being in sync with the communities in which our businesses reside as well as understanding and valuing the needs of the consumers.

There is enough to go around--if we are not so greedy as to hoard the extras. And, in this equation of socially conscious businesses, the industry that society has labeled as "not for profit; nonprofit and 501c3" organizations, have the opportunity to lead the way.

These organizations understand the cause and affect of giving and the strong and steady heartbeat began at their formulation of *giving* as a means of *operating*. Yet, 501c3's have not competently expressed a positive fit in this equation. As the only industry that is described by what *is "not" done verses what "is" done*, we are often forced into spaces of lack, contrary to the on-purpose services and products offered. Eventually, our organizations appear as poor and needy (just as much in need as the constituents served).

With this impoverished mentality it is no wonder the difficulty nonprofits have in acquiring funds for mainly excellent services provided for society to work more holistically.

My work in this space, encourages organizations providing on-purpose services to stand up for their work with a stronger heartbeat, embracing titles that better inform the work. Changing the labels, help build stronger infrastructure and empower our entire community -- affiliates, employees, constituents and donors. As you read these works note "nonprofit" and "not-for-profit" is replaced by "social profit" or "on purpose".

This is my own personal way of correcting the skip in the heartbeat of the service community. This is the beginning of the shift being encouraged.

Join me in uplifting the powerful work of Social Profit Organizations as positive and inspiring, by choosing our words carefully and specifically focus towards making a difference.

Chapter One
Building Your Case

Bathroom: Each fixture has a specific name for a specific reason.

Business: What words do you use to describe your organization?

The bathroom is full of fixtures. Faucets, sinks, vanity lighting, regular lighting, showerheads, mirrors, bathtub, toilet, towel rings and floor mats. Each fixture serves a purpose and is identified clearly with what it is or does. A tissue holder is designed to hold tissue paper while a floor mat covers the floor and keeps you from stepping on a slippery surface.

In the bathroom it's pretty simple, and there are colorful descriptors to convince consumers to purchase those fixtures. In the Social Profit world, we must use a metaphor of colorful fixtures as well. Our stories must include engaging words and descriptors that showcase what and how we do what we do.

Supporters need to see the story – even if they are not physically present and, they need to understand the "why" in order to be fully committed to support your cause.

Change your words and change your money

How you speak and write about your organization tells your audience more than just the work you are doing. It also tells where you stand in the community landscape. It may sound "hokey" but *positive words bring positive results*.

When organizations speak uplifting words regarding their organization, the energy is transferred to outsiders and draws them into participate. Even when the community situation is bleak, speaking into the possibilities of a situation is much more powerful than just rehashing what's already in existence.

Ever had someone invite you to an event or party with the preface that it was going to be boring, old fashioned, no fun, out of date, expensive or dull? Sometimes it sounds like this:

"Jane I have tickets to this event. Last time I went it was long and there were no men to choose from. The music sucked and the speakers were boring. I would have fallen asleep but there weren't enough chairs to sit in so I had to stand all night. Want to go with me this year?"

What do you think Jane is going to say? My guess is the answer will begin with an "N" and end with a big fat "O" AND there may be an explanative attached! No one wants to attend or participate in something that has no benefit. And negative messaging is not a draw.

Donors and volunteers feel the same way. When you give all the negatives of your organization, it weighs people down so that they don't have the energy to participate.

Equip your organization with information about the good work that you're doing. Tell about the people who already support you (even if they are few and far between). Share the work that's going on and the work that you envision. Yes, tell the story of where you started but make sure it includes where you are headed. Begin writing your successes in quantitative and qualitative form. Share that information along with an invitation for people to join you in the good work that you're doing.

People want to be inspired and uplifted. They want to be part of something that's working. They want to be a part of something that matters. Change your words to *powerful* words that matter verses *weak* words that make you mope. In the bathroom scenario we would highlight how the bathroom mat matches the shower curtain before talking about how wet the floor became because neither the mat nor curtain worked.

Tell your story so that it enhances your donor's experience. Yes, it's important that your donor understands the problems you face, but it's also important for them to understand the successes that you have. Even more critical is that they know what their money will do to enhance your constituent's experience.

Creating Your Story

Creating a compelling story for your social profit is also known as creating a *Case for Support*. In the book, People and Programs Social Profit Biz Basics, a scenario for building a better case for support was presented. In that book it reviewed how programs were better organized understanding what they were designed to do. In addition to understanding your organization's programs and overall goals, stories also help with how to market and raise money for the organization. As you define your organization and your programs, be certain the words used lead to building culture and brand for all that you do.

Working with programs, leaders learn quickly that documenting everything allows the creation of a methodology to the work being conducted. The methodology is part of your case for support. It describes what you do, how you do it and why—all within the context of programs and projects. Methodologies, when combined with surveys also provide evaluative measurements that can help build on your case for support. Informing those outside the program of quantitative and qualitative data on the work that your program does is invaluable.

Understanding not only what and how services occur, but also why and where the impact occurs, supports your story with a strong beginning, middle and end. These type stories formulate the making of a great story around programs and the administration. The culmination of the programs, staff and client stories help create a strong and compelling organizational case for support.

So how do you tell your story? Is it only in the mission statement or is it expanded into a vision as well? An expanded case for support includes the mission, value and vision of your organization. It is how you tell what you do and how you do it. It is also, quite frankly, good storytelling!

Consider the thousands of social profits that are in existence today. Each is needed in the world as much as the next. One may sound similar to the next but truly each has a unique way of contributing their work into the world.

What is your unique proposition for contributing to the world? Do you feed the hungry? How do you do it differently than the others that serve the same purpose? Do you offer shelter? What is different about your location? Is your service with youth? What do you do with them and how does it stand apart from the hundreds of other Boys and Girls Clubs or Youth Centers across the country?

When you figure out your unique proposition, it's the start to sharing your story.

Part of what makes you different of course, is the people that administer the program. Accent the quality of your team in your case for support. If you have people with stellar academics and education is a core element of what you do, mention the qualifications of those who work with you. On the same note, if the program is for a trade and you have certified technicians administering the program, that becomes a unique feature as well.

What is most important is that you find the key areas that are unique to you. It could be your founder and it could be in the population you serve. Perhaps you are the only organization serving black spotted cats. This makes you unique as your market space is narrow and specific.

Many people believe that being too focused or specific in their market is a hindrance because they will not be eligible for the broad range of funding that is available. In some cases, this may be true (not sure if you'll find a ton of donors for Black Spotted Cats) but narrowing your market is essential to secure a

15

solid donor base. When your organization has a specific goal that is uniquely for you, it allows for you to find the right donors to become unique involved.

Cat lovers will be interested in joining organizations that specifically work with cats while those who want to work with children, may not be as interested in cats. Combining children and cats in your mission might garner you support from both populations, but be careful that it doesn't also cause additional problems with your constituents and cost more than the combination is worth.

For the Cat and Youth organization example above, you will need specific insurances, team members and facilities for both populations and they will have to be separate in many cases. Liability increases as you add general areas into your programs and again, though you are open to more funders (cat lovers and youth lovers) you are also open to many more problems.

Get specific in your programming and don't stray. The problems and complications are not worth the potential of additional donors.

Chapter Two
Sharing the Message

Bathroom: Want to find a bathroom? Look for the familiar RESTROOM brand.

Business: Business messages should be easily identifiable with your brand.

When you go to a mall, a party or any event, one of the inevitable searches becomes finding the bathroom. It's usually in a pretty obvious place that's not so obvious because it's tucked away where no one can see!

At outdoor venues, bathroom stalls (or porta potties) are usually found on the outskirts of the event. Indoors they can be found at entrances and exits in most cases. No matter where the bathroom is located, there are signs and postings indicating their location. Additionally, those hosting and participating with the facility or event are all well aware of the restroom locations and amenities. The bathroom becomes one of the most important parts of a business venture or event because it's the one place everyone has a common need for.

Knowing about your bathroom and where it's located is about proper signage and information and in the social profit world, knowing about your organization is called branding and marketing.

A clear definition of branding taken from the Free Dictionary on-line states: *The process of creating differentiation between a product and other products of the same kind. Branding is a marketing strategy to create the impression that one product is better than the other, whether or not that is true. Branding makes a product more recognizable and therefore is likely to attract customers and customer loyalty.*

For our purposes in the social profit sector branding is creating an emotional connection with stakeholders. We don't focus so much on competition as in the for profit world, because when everyone is working for the common good, competition is eliminated. I firmly believe that there is enough for everyone participating in this space and that nothing that one organization receives is counter productive for another. Each organization is given in the manner in which they asks and to what they need.

This is a challenging belief system as grants and contests push social profits to participate as if they are competing for the only dollars available. In fact, there is plenty and abundance should organizations begin to pool efforts and expand their consciousness in how these setups are designed. In this book we will use the expanded philosophy of plenty and focus on making sure organizations are uniquely designed to attract loyal donors.

How do you brand and market your organization? Do you have literature that tells our story? Are your business cards and stationary consistent with your message and brochure? And how is your culture, impacted by the branding of the organization?

Marketing Starts With Your Brand

Branding is not marketing or advertising, but it is the key to selling your organization to potential supporters. Branding starts with a strong case for support that articulates your key messages about your organization. The organization's identity, constituents and unique proposition is part of your branding strategy – which means this should be part of your case for support. This information then must be shared with a unified and consistent voice.

Messages created in this vein more readily resonate with stakeholders. As a social profit organization leader, you know your ultimate goals are to receive funding, volunteer support and have happy constituents utilizing your services. How you state this end result in terms of your objectives and outcomes is imperative.

I suggest social profits create a brand strategy, much like that of corporations. We all have heard and seen the strategies across the board – from the Nike swish and tag, "just do it" to Starbucks mermaid signifying the beauty of their coffee with the green color indicating growth. Starbuck's uses taglines to differentiate their products too, like their campaign, *"Starbucks Double Shot. Bring on the Day."* Whether you are a big company or a small social profit, it's important to do your homework when solidifying your brand. To create a brand strategy for your social profit, consider the following process of venting things out and including others:

1. Conduct a SWOT Analysis and review it for brand messaging opportunities. SWOT is the acronym for Strengths, Weaknesses, Opportunities and Threats. Using team members from every department and at all levels (including board members) is the most effective way to do a SWOT Analysis.

2. Ask questions of your team to engage the process so that you understand what makes your organization work well. An example of questions for each section of the SWOT are: *Strengths:* What do you do best? How do donors view you? How do clients view you? What distinguishes you from others like you? *Weaknesses:* What is unclear to your audience(s)? How much does the team or the board know about our current brand? *Opportunities:* Is there a market for what we offer? Where can we fill in within our community landscape? *Threats:* Are there external factors that keep us from promoting ourselves? Who else is in this space and how effective are they?

3. Next review with your team what

you've learned about the organization, what it does, how it's done and why anyone should care. These messages will help you figure out what your brand should center around. Once you review, determine the messages your audience should be presented. What you think the audience should hear is not always what they need to hear.

4. After reviewing, rewrite and have a review with some outsiders. Once they've given their input use valuable feedback to complete your plan. Remember when getting feedback you are not asking this final group of people to create a campaign for you -- you are asking them for real reactions as to whether the message was delivered as you intended. You want to know if the words and phrases impacted this group of people in the way you meant it to. You do not want them to recreate your brand strategy.

Do not assume that that the message you put together is wrong or right. This is where the feedback is invaluable. Your real question is whether the campaign resonates

Thyonne Gordon, Ph.D

with your intended audience. This step is important as many times leaders assume the information is correct because they are so entrenched in the process. Do not make assumptions. Listen to the people that the message is for – your clients who are served, your volunteers and your donors. If the message is not clear to those that you already have, then it won't be clear when recruiting new people.

Branding is an essential part of the marketing process. Take a look at some organizations that do it well and see if you can replicate on ideas that they have used. Well-branded social profits include: American Red Cross, Boys & Girls Clubs and the Salvation Army. When you think of these organizations names, there are certain feelings and images that come to mind immediately. Perhaps a Santa ringing a bell during the holidays or a catastrophic event with emergency carts rolling through come to mind. The point is, these organizations conjure an image of what they do and leave a positive feeling that you can trust them to do just what is in your head right now. You want your organization to have a brand message that feels just as powerful.

Branding Is For the Big Boys – NOT!

The importance of your brand can't be emphasized enough. We know this because of McDonald's, Mercedes and Apple. Yet, many times social profits play small in thinking it doesn't pertain to them. If you are one of those organizations with the belief that messaging is only for the big boys – then you are sadly mistaken.

Branding is the key element to your message being in the minds of the audience population that you want. When you are not clear with your messaging – or your brand – you cannot get a clear connection to the audience you are trying to reach. Your brand is the heart of your organization. It is like the soul to your personality or in bathroom language, it's the toilet to the seat! Think about the bathroom analogy. If you had a toilet seat but no container attached, you would have a great big mess!

Doing the work of your social profit is not enough -- you have to tell people about your good work. Social Profit professionals do the work for the love of the work or the cause – not for the glory or bragging rights making branding feel opposite to the nature of the

social profit industry. Nevertheless, the brand
you create will sell your organization to
supporters.

That's right I used a profit word – *sell*. I
use this word because that's what every
business does to get customers in some form or
fashion. In the social profit world, you are
selling the idea of helping or servicing others.
You are selling the idea that if donors and
supporters gave their time and money, you
could continue doing what you do and perhaps
even do more of it. Your messaging is just as
much a sales pitch than the sale of shoes at
Macy's. The biggest difference is you have the
ability to affect massive change in your sell,
because you are convincing a variety of
audiences that what you are doing is so
valuable that you can't put a profit price on it.

Use your stories, photos and leaders to
differentiate your brand. When you establish an
emotional connection with your constituents, it
connects and keeps them close to you. Make
your brand clear, powerful and meaningful so
that when others hear it, the effectiveness rings
clear.

Getting the Message Out – Marketing 101

So once you have a brand what's next? It's time to get the word out and let the world know about what you're doing. How you do this can be relatively simple and inexpensive. Marketing is a special dance where each party dances to the beat. Both donor and organizational needs are satisfied in a successful marketing strategy. Finally, stronger relationships are established. Below are the top elements for a successful marketing campaign.

1. *Create a clear brand.* Well, there you have it—the first half of this book presented the key component of your marketing strategy. In your brand understand your constituents and communicate to them. Measure the work based on their feedback and fine tune your programs. When you are ***clear*** you will be able to present your brand through the services you provide. Regular and consistent brand messages generate a reputation and give your organization a personality, which will help create brand awareness and ultimately support.

2. *Write it down.* Documentation is key in

branding and marketing for consistency. Even if team members have a different feel in how to communicate a message, the words should be the same. If your organization chooses to adapt to the movement of Social Profit verbiage then negative words will be eliminated from the vocabulary. "At-risk youth" become "at-promise youth" perhaps living in at risk conditions. Know your messages by writing them down. Post them on the walls of your organization, in brochures, partly on business cards and on the website. Your words must be consistent.

3. *Leverage Social Media.* While the world is filled with people who like a variety of things, it's your job to engage those who are interested in what you do. Share your message through social media with compelling stories of your organization and highlight the overall sector in which you serve. If you work with animals, share industry stats in your social media – not just.

4. *Know & Participate In Your*

Community. Once you know your case for support, include community outings as part of your brand marketing strategy. Your community landscape is vital for your sustainability. Get to know your political officers. Public officials job is to serve their constituents and your organization is a major part of that so make sure they know you and the importance of the work you do to aid the community they shepherd. This support will become reciprocal as you are both servicing the same constituents. Attend community forums and remember, as you participate find others who can support your sharing through social media giving "shout outs" to everyone.

5. *Define and Know Your Target Market.* Whether by researching similar organizations or finding out through the census, know whom you are serving so that you can create a better case. Many nonprofits say they serve, "everyone". That is just not true. Your service needs to be clear and you need a target market. Yes, it's okay to make exceptions to this market when offering

service. If you are a food bank only serving women and a young child comes in hungry – of course you will find a way to feed him or her. However, know your target audience and stick with it. Your supporters want something that they consistently care about. Choose a market the same way your donors choose a cause – and then own it. Once you know your market and you've taken ownership determine the desired outcomes of your marketing efforts to them.

6. *Create appealing marketing materials.* Your marketing materials should be targeted towards your market. This includes your website presence, brochures, business cards, press releases and anything that goes out about your organization. Notice how Breast Cancer Awareness stays with the color "pink." There are men who have breast cancer but the campaign's target market is women -- so everything they do is catered towards women giving consistency in messaging.

Money & Marketing: Social Profit Biz Basics

These marketing basics should get you well on the way with creating a marketing strategy. Most important is to be consistent with whatever area you focus on. Should you not be able to do all of the marketing suggestions at once because of limited time or staffing, then don't! Choose one and be consistent. It's better to stay focused on Twitter weekly than to create Instagram, Pinterest, Facebook, LinkedIn, Vine and a host of others and only use them once. Consistency is key.

Marketing Through Social Media and Websites

In today's digital world, just about every business is connected to some digital format. Having a website is key to operating and having your message readily available for potential supporters. Social media has also become a huge portal for sending and receiving messages of support. Some guidelines for these two platforms follow.

Creating A Powerful Website

Websites share useful information, news, monthly newsletters, events and ways to donate. Your website is your opportunity to showcase your organization so make it professional and easy to use.

1. *Easy & clear navigation.* It's important that visitors to your site can move through it easily without hiccups. Create a site that allows users to move fluidly through the pages without confusion.

2. *Interesting and compelling content should be first.* Strong images help build connections that are different than with words alone. Use videos and photos.

3. *Create a friendly social media platform on your site.* Every page of your site should include social sharing links. Make it easy for videos, photo sharing and bloggers to embed images and profiles to attract new traffic sources, retain visitors, and build community around your cause.

4. *See your site through another's eyes.* Pretend to be a first time visitor to your site and see if you receive the messages

you intended for your visitor. Are the actions you want a visitor to take clear and easy to understand? Surveys are a great way to make your site dynamic and gauge the site's usability. Use a service like Survey Monkey for an inexpensive survey set up.

5. *Email sign-up must be prominent and easy.* Maintaining regular and meaningful contact with people who have already shown an interest can be done with an email newsletter. This will also help build your list and strengthen relationships. It's also easier to collect emails if you provide interesting content in return.

6. *Use powerful and compelling messages on your home page.* Make sure your words are accurate and descriptive. If you only had ten words to describe your organization, what would those words be? Also use words that mirror the keywords and phrases people are likely to use searching for you or your issues.

7. *Prominently feature your 'Donate Now' button.* A Donate button doesn't

guarantee anyone will use it but it certainly increases your odds and assures visitors don't have to think about ways to engage with you. Having a compelling story and showing visitors how you want them to engage will make it easy for visitors to support you.

8. *Show your contact information.* Even in this high tech world, the best way to build a relationship is to show them that you are real. Phone numbers and addresses build trust and a sense of accessibility and these items are often content people are looking for when they go to your site.

9. *Limit the number of "clicks" visitors need to get your message.* The rule of thumb is, "three clicks and you're out." Make sure the first message you want to get across is no more than three clicks away. Research indicates that you lose 40% of visitors with each click.

10. *Use tools to build and test your search functions.* Tools such as Google

Analytics will tell you if users are finding what they need on your site. A search function and site map is a quick and easy way to help users get to their destination as quickly as possible.

11. *Blog connections are important.* A blog is an effective way to share your latest news and online engagement. Think of your blog as your website's friend. However, only start a blog if you have something to say and can commit to a regular schedule. Blogging will also help raise your search engine ratings.

Chapter Three
Securing Your Donor Base

Bathroom: With all the fixtures and appliances, bathrooms don't work without water.

Business: The organization and the programs can be fantastic but without the funding, they are not sustainable. What is your water source?

Imagine having the perfect bathroom, with the perfect sink, sunken bathtub, two waterfall showerheads in a double sized shower, which is fully equipped with a steam feature. Imagine that this bathroom has a perfect welcoming bright color and the toilet seat has a warming device, so that when you take a seat on it – you really feel like you're on a throne. There's even a European bidet next to the toilet – for the perfect after use cleanse. All of this and alas, NO WATER!

Your bathroom is pretty nice but without water, it's useless. So why bother to have all

these extra amenities if you can't use them –
because you don't have water? That's a
question I ask a lot and not just about
bathrooms, but in general with items we
consume in life. If you can't gas up a Rolls
Royce, do you really need one? If you have no
means of paying an electric, gas and water bill
should you have a house? And the one that
really baffles me, why have a Satellite Dish if
you can't buy a television?

Believe it or not, all of the above scenarios
happen every day – and more frequently than
you might think. What also happens every day
is social profit founders, who are visionary,
vibrant and dedicated to their causes, create
organizations and have no idea of how, when,
where or who will fund them. It is this mind set
of beginning 501c3's that I ask every founder to
challenge BEFORE beginning a new social
profit.

So how do you meet the challenge of
wanting to do good but not having the funds to
do so? Well, you've started in the right place by
just thinking about the question. When we put
the hard issues right in front of us, there's often
a solution that's easier than we think.

Let's start with the person who's running your fundraising. Normally, the founder begins this work since they have the passion for the cause. As a fundraiser, this leader is personable and gives voice to the cause. Even if they are not personable in a pleasant way, whatever is put forth from the fundraising leader is a clear message about why the work needs to be done. There have been angry fundraisers who are so disgusted by a particular condition that their passion comes across as strong anger and in that anger they are fighting for their causes' right no exist. This can work – but is limited to causes whee justice comes into play like the Civil Rights movement. Most leaders in fundraising are pleasant and personable exuding an authentic energy about the cause they passionately support.

So who is leading your fundraising efforts? Make sure they enjoy it and are clear with why they are sharing the cause with donors. Founders are usually clear on the cause but often confused in the ask that they are making to their perspective donor. Not only are they in a relationship with the organization and understanding its' nuances but they are in a relationship with every person they meet who may be a potential donor.

Because Founders are often more focused on programs and services, they might consider hiring a good Development (or fundraising) person as the first hire. Good fundraisers are worth their weight in gold because they love the work of the organization but even more they love finding ways to make sure the work continues. This means they finding the money (or the water) so the organization can sustain.

The job of a fundraiser is to know their perspective and current donors. It is a relationship dance and the funder is leading -- without letting the donor know he's in the lead. These fundraisers know how to make people really like them. Seriously! They remember birthdays, children's activities, and everything that's important to their important donors. They do not take any donor for granted and they are on top of their game – enjoying the work that they do. These funders know that the work they do sustains the work of the organization that they do it for. Their mission is just as strong as the core mission of the institution. In short, good fundraisers are good with people.

The Money Challenge Is Really The People Challenge

We see that funding or money is the source of water for social profits to exist. The challenges that come head on with most organizations in this space continue to present the same

- Lack of funding
- Lack of time
- Lack of resources
- Lack of people

Even though these perceived "lacks" continue to surface, social profits have a hard time identifying why. One reason for these "lacks" is because social profits don't plan accordingly to fill the lack. By assuring the right people are in place, the other lacks become non-existent. Think about it. If you had the right people to raise money – there would be no lack of funding or resources. When those people have the proper resources, they can manage their time better. Looks like bringing in the right people and communicating properly with people is the best way to get funded.

Money & Marketing: Social Profit Biz Basics

What do you think makes you buy from one place verses another? People buy from people and places they know and trust. Donors are people who give to causes and people that they like.

You buy your morning latte at LaLa's Latte Central because LaLa greets you by name when you walk in and knows exactly how you like your latte. You shop at Mike's Deli, a local spot, because the staff is friendly and helpful and because you like Mike. He's a nice guy.

The same principle applies to raising money. People give to the people and the causes that they like. Whether it's a multi-millionaire, grants officer or an employee at a corporation – your chances of getting funded by any of them increase considerably when you have a healthy personal relationship with the potential contributor. Want the odds to get even greater? Schedule a face-to-face meeting and your chances of getting support double! This process of building relationships is called one-to-one fundraising.

Why Focus on One to One Fundraising?

We ask our Development person to do just about everything. Write grants, stories, press releases, track data, evaluate, send grant reports, thank the volunteers, recruit the volunteers, and make sure everyone got the proper thank you and holiday card at the end of the year. It's impossible for one person to do all of those things and be effective. Still, more often than not, they are charged with these tasks – and they do their best to fulfill the challenge. So where's the focus? It's nowhere! And when the focus is nowhere – the money follows suit and is NO WHERE!

The most effective way to raise money is through one to one fundraising. It's been proven with data, statistics and real life scenarios. So why don't we allow our development people the time to do just that? Why are they not meeting with donors and watering the relationship? Why are they not at lunches and dinners and coffee meetings assuring that each person is treated like an individual campaign?

The answer is simple. Social profits operate out of lack and can only see what's directly in front of them. When leaders of these wonderful organizations don't see the money right in front of them there's often a panic feeling. In panic we operate in mayhem. First there's a grant opportunity that pops up (that we may or may not be qualified for) but it's in front of us so we jump on it. All efforts are put into the completion of that grant and in the process, we neglect the people who have already supported us. A contest appears next and all hands on deck to enter. There is such a sporadic sense of how to raise funds in many social profits such that nothing is consistent and messaged properly.

When social profits get out of their own way and allow development professionals to do the most important thing first, they can then benefit from the seeds being planted and watered with a fresh crop of funds.

This doesn't mean grants, corporate support and events to raise funds are not important. It only means the organization must prioritize what is most important. And in doing so, revenue may be slow coming in, but sustainable and lasting in the long run.

Thyonne Gordon, Ph.D

Meeting with potential and current donors in one on one settings give donors a chance to see and feel the passion embedded in the organization. These meetings provide an intimate opportunity to build trust and allegiance to your brand in a way that even the best DVD, website or brochure cannot do.

More than 80 percent of social profit funding comes from individuals and foundations. Of that 80 percent, the majority of the funding was acquired from one on one meetings. With those odds, why not support one on one meetings as the priority?

Understand Who You're Dealing With

Various terms are used for different campaigns and donors. One term that was introduced earlier is that of a Major Gift Donor. This is a term used for a person who has given a significant gift to the organization. Your budget and you determine a significant gift.

Significant gifts vary in amounts. For one person it is $100 and another $10,000. You create the categories of funding for your donor base. When contemplating your major gift category consider your budget and what your constituents have given in the past. This category is the most effective means of receiving "big money" gifts.

Meeting in person with each donor is the start of a personal connection forming long term giving. It is through an effective fundraiser finding out the interest of the donor connection to the organization verses the money – that you build a winning combination.

As an early stage social profit, the thought is that because of limited resources there is no time to court individuals. This is exactly the time that you need to build relationships with one on one attention. Remember more than 80 percent of all giving to social profits comes from individuals. I will repeat this message over and over because again, it is the most important lesson one can learn in fundraising.

From this lesson it should be deduced that the winning formula for maximizing the return on your fundraising professional's efforts is through intimate one-to-one meetings with current and perspective donors. Eighty percent of your fundraising teams' time must be in cultivating relationships and making in person, personal, appeals in order to be successful.

Other fundraising tactics, such as direct mail and events, are effective when done with expertise. However, they should be used as add-ons to the main tactic of building relationships and connections. And when using them remember to keep the ratio of time committed to such projects at a minimal. Why? Because they return a minimal percentage to your portfolio.

Also note that many times other activities can be very profitable but they have been employed with skilled professionals and costly resources that can be prohibitive for beginning or intermediate sized social profits. When there is a large marketing and fundraising budgets coupled with an extensive mailing list – then it's time to explore additional means of outreach.

Early stage social profits are not in a position to have these luxuries. And even if there were a miraculous gift to employ such resources, I stand by the fact that individuals do 80 percent of the giving and therefore the majority of your time should be spent with individuals in small settings.

I know I'm over emphasizing this point but I implore you to decipher the equation and really bring it to its core. If you can raise 80 percent of your money by doing just 2-3 things, and two of those things rank highest on effectiveness, why would you bother with anything else first?

Creating a fundraising campaign

Just like piping the plumbing in the bathroom to make sure your water flows, it's important to plan out how you plan on flowing in your cash!. So let's talk about effective campaigns. Obviously, with my emphasis on understanding the importance of individual giving – that's the main type of campaign discussed in this book. Campaigns come in many forms. There are capital campaigns to raise money for building; event campaigns to raise money for special events; planned giving campaigns to raise money based on bequests, trusts and wills (or departing gifts) and there are Individual and Major Gift Donor campaigns to raise money from people that we know or will get to know. We're going to focus on Individual and Major Gift Donors.

This type of campaign is a standard customer relationship database campaign. Because everyone you know is an individual, it starts with just that—listing the people that you know. As you list these people, you will begin to categorize them in different giving platforms. Start with the people who have already supported you and build from there. Once you develop your list you can begin categorizing what a "major gift" is for your organization. Whether 10 or 1000 people are in your database, you will begin a campaign to reach every single person with a targeted message. Let's go through some of the steps to begin your campaign.

Identify and qualify your donor base

Know your existing donors, what their giving level is and where they fall in your individual and major gift giving campaign.

One way to figure out a major gift category is calculate 1% of the total budget. Other ways are to find the highest donor median in your database and use that. You might also use the highest amount you've ever received from any donor and start there.

As you go through your database, look for your diamonds in the rough. These are folks who've presented well with nice gifts and support and are bursting with potential to do more. Use these people as indicators of what your major donor looks like and begin cultivating the relationships. Write notes about your donor – from their passions and family history to their ability to give and connections. As you identify more information about your donors, you will begin to know them better and perhaps even identify with them on various levels.

Define your donor list categories based on donation sizes. It's important that this process be as simple as tracking them on an Excel sheet with the ability to sort different columns. Keep your donor list simple and divided into donation size categories (i.e. $100; $500; $1000; $5000; $10,000 and so on). When you sort through the numbers you will find a median or average number that stands out. That is your core donor base.

"Major gift donor" is a category that's defined clearly in the social profit world but other donors are often clumped together. To give specific messages to your donors try labeling donors based on the categories you've established.

- Program Supporters: $1 - $1,000
- Program Creators: $1,001 - $5,000
- Program Sustainers: $5,001 - $9,999
- Major Gift Donor: $10,000+

I don't have a list...

When you don't have a list, it's time to start speaking with people and recruiting supporters so that you have one. Start with your board members and staff. Extend the list to your volunteers, vendors and business associates. Anyone that you know can be added to your preliminary list. If they have not given anything to you, based on your knowledge of the person make a guess on what they can give. You may have a potential diamond in the rough in your court and you're not recognizing it.

As you grow your organization and enter your donor prospects, you will learn more about your donors and this familiarity will go a long way with prospects in building relationships.

Meeting and Greeting Your Prospects

Once you establish your supporter base, it's time to get to know them. You may invite everyone out to a gathering to showcase your work and then have an appeal (or ask) at the end. Or you may want to set up meetings with each person individually to speak with them about the great work that you see possible having them in your corner. They know about your work (I hope) and now they need to know that you want to know more about them. The meeting should be simple and can be at a coffee shop, over lunch or right in your offices where programs can be apparent.

Let your meeting be light and carefree. This is a meeting for you to get information more than giving information. You want to learn who is using your bathroom and what they need. Let the potential donor know that you just want to spend some time with them to get to know them better. You may even share that your intention IS NOT to ask for money. And when the meeting happens, be enthusiastic about your mission but also probe to find common connection and enthusiasm for your potential donor. Find out what makes them tick.

Final pointers for meeting your donors:

1. Be passionate and prepared to answer questions and share about yourself as well as the organization.
2. Be personable and get personal.
3. Use humor and be light and centered.
4. Control the tempo, tone and the topics that you discuss.
5. Respect the time frame and keep it under an hour

Follow up with your meeting with emails, cards or notes. Schedule additional meetings and if there's something you can include their family in, do that. At your follow up meetings, it's okay to get into more detail about the organization and its' needs. Still, gather facts on what connects this person with your organization and show them how the connection could work. As you deepen the relationship you will be strengthening the emotional connection to the work and mission of what you do.

Money & Marketing: Social Profit Biz Basics

How To Ask For What You Want

At the end of the day, it all comes down to asking for what you want. It's easy for some people to ask for anything, but in this industry where every cause needs a champion, leaders often become a bit timid in asking for what they want. Instead they beg for what they need and come across as desperate.

That is not the image that a social profit in the line of doing important work needs to have. There should be a sense of pride in being a part of this industry and if I might be so bold as to say, an edge of arrogance that the work being done is vital for the survival of our communities.

Don't take this out of context. It is important to show humility and gratitude as it is equally important to be passionate and proud of the nature of the work that is being done in your organization. There's no need to cower or beg for support. This is work that is noble and commands respect so when asking for money keep these things in mind:

1. Have I equipped my potential donor with all the information they need to make an informed decision on giving?
2. Has this person seen the programs we offer through literature or other media messaging as well as in person?
3. Have I answered the tough questions they had in an effective manner?
4. Did I do my homework on who this person is so that I know the right questions to ask them?

If you answer "yes" to all of the questions above, then you are prepared to make a comfortable ask to your donor. Not only will you be comfortable but it will be okay for your donor too. When you're prepared you already know this person; what they're capable of and you know that they are interested in your cause.

Now, if you read here and say, "Well, I know who they are and they're not really interested in the cause, but I know them very well and want to ask for a donation." That's a slippery slope. Yes, you want your friends to support you regardless of their interest, but wouldn't it be even better if they "got it?" If this person was connected to the cause for any reason, do you think their gift would be more significant? Absolutely!

When cultivating your donors, spend time on the ones who "get it." That doesn't mean leave out those who show mediocrity. However, you don't want to spend a lot of time with folks who really don't want to spend a lot of time with you! Make sure you're asking the right person for the right amount and you can be sure you will have success. When you have the right person, they will be honored you asked them to participate.

When it doesn't work?

I've been asked when "the ask" doesn't work. There is a scenario in which this can happen. I guess I'll go back to the bathroom to explain.

The water in the bathroom at our social profit was not working. It had been off for the full day. After checking all services to assure we were still connected and timely on the bill, I began trouble shooting other places. I checked every bathroom to see if the water was on. Nothing was running. It was all dried up and I

Thyonne Gordon, Ph.D

had no idea what to do. We closed the center that day because there was a problem. As I was walking with security to shut down, I ran into our maintenance guy and told him we were going to close the center because the water was off. He said "Okay."

I continued the process of clearing the place and just as I was leaving for the day I saw the maintenance man again and told him we need to figure out the water supply. He asked me, "Do you want me to turn it on?"

In an incredulous, mouth drop, I looked at him and said, "What?"

"Do you want me to turn it on?" he asked again.

I said, "Yes…." And he proceeded to walk out the room to the main water line, switching it on.

"Why didn't you tell me that it could be turned on from that valve?" I asked.

His response was, "You didn't ask me."

The moral of the story is to *Just Ask!* Fundraising work when we don't ask. We don't ask for what we need. We don't ask for what we want. We don't ask for anything. When we don't ask, we don't get funded.

Other ways to get funded

There are many ways to raise money for your social profit. Social profits are known for events, drives, marathons and other activities to raise awareness and funds. Have a plan for whatever you want to do in fundraising. If it is 4 appeals a year, time them out properly and begin the process early. If it's an event, make sure that the income exceeds the expenses. Whatever you do, have a plan of action and a team to make it happen.

Many times, organizations can increase their funds without doing a lot of intensive work. Matching gift opportunities is one way to do this. As you are working on building relationships, find a donor who may challenge others to do a matching gift campaign. Major gift donors love these opportunities because it's a way that they encourage others to make their gift even more substantial. Once a challenge is put out there, people can respond without you having to go to each one directly for the same ask.

Confidence In Good Times and Bad

No matter how much homework you do, there are still going to be some objections to giving. It comes with the territory. I look at each "no" as a step towards my "yes" because that's how the law of averages works. Still, it can be deflating to be sure that someone is going to say yes to an appeal and they end up saying no. Don't take it personal. Explore why the answer is no. Sometimes people have not shared circumstances that are beyond their control. Other times they have just been overly nice but actually have another cause they support heavily. Whatever the case, it's valuable intel for you in your future relationship building.

Know that if you've done your homework, most rejections to participate are because the timing is off or the donor is not in a position to give. However, these very people are respectful of how you handle the rejection and will often return with something or someone to replace what the organization lost in them.

Money & Marketing: Social Profit Biz Basics

Whether you have a good or bad experience, take it in stride and know that the work you are doing matters. In the end you must celebrate. You made it this far so celebrate. You have met new people and learned new things. Celebrate. You are part of important work. Celebrate. You have impacted the masses. Celebrate.

Take with you a sense of satisfaction that your work is paramount to community and in all that you do you've met giving and caring people who keep that work going.

Time to match the mission with the money and market yourself into success!

Chapter Four
In Summary

Bathroom: Connected to our water source & maintaining the stalls keeps this bathroom working for all!

Business: Once we connect the mission to the money, we passionately keep the organization alive.

There was a lot to cover in the Money and Marketing book! Building your case is so important when it comes to explaining what you do. Remember to use powerful words and phrases for your social profit. It's not just the leaders that have to do this. Every team member needs to know the consistent message that you will share.

As you gather stories of your social profit's work, include successes and failures. Many times people are afraid to share the things that didn't work – but these incidents are just as invaluable as those things that work. These obstacles help us strive to do better and show us problems that need to be solved.

Share your message through a variety of mediums including brochures, websites and flyers. When it comes to building out your social media, seek expert advice. It will take you further than you think. Your cause is important so use the stories that you've gathered to build your case to let people know of the significance of your work.

Finally, securing your donors can only be done once you've achieved consistent ways to bather your story, build your case and share the information. Once you have that solid, reaching out to donors and potential donors to participate with your programs will be much easier. You can direct them to your website or to a recently posted blog through social media. As you grow your donor base, your materials will develop and grow as well.

Use your resources wisely and maximize on the time it takes to fundraise. Do this by understanding which fundraising techniques work best. We've said it over and over – one on one fundraising is key. When you don't have time or money – the most efficient and effective way to raise money is to meet with donors face to face.

In closing, I wish you the best in your fundraising endeavors and know that following the simple techniques in this book will take you a long way.